An Exploration of

The Tetons

Featuring text from
"The Ascent of Mount Hayden," 1873
by Nathaniel P. Langford

FARCOUNTRY
PRESS

photography by David William Peterson

ISBN 10: 1-56037-303-2
ISBN 13: 978-1-56037-303-2

For more information on our books, write Farcountry Press,
P.O. Box 5630,Helena, MT 59604; call (800) 821-3874;
or visit www.farcountrypress.com.

Created, produced, and designed in the United States.

Printed in China.

15 14 13 12 11 10   3 4 5 6 7

In 1870, Nathaniel Pitt Langford was a member of the Washburn-Doane Yellowstone Expedition and kept a journal of the adventure, later published as *The Discovery of Yellowstone Park*. 1872, Langford accompanied another expedition to the Yellowstone area, this time approaching from the southwest and traveling through what would become Grand Teton National Park.

Langford published a narrative of his second visit, "The Ascent of Mount Hayden: A New Chapter of Western Discovery," in 1873 in *Scribner's Monthly*, Volume VI, pages 129–157. Reproduced here are pages 129–147, with minor typographic adjustments.

The "Mount Hayden" in this narrative is the Grand Teton, which Langford proposed to name in honor of Dr. Ferdinand V. Hayden, leader of the U.S. Geological Survey expedition of which this Teton exploration was part. The ascent of the Grand Teton by Langford and James Stevenson was thought to be the first successful climb of this peak by non-natives.

Left: Moulton barn, with Middle and Grand Teton to the northwest.

Title page: Eastern flank of Mt. Moran.

Front cover: String Lake.

3

Mt. Woodring and Mt. Moran from the Oxbox Bend of the Snake River.

Cascade Canyon sunset from Spread Creek.

STEVENSON IN PERIL

The Ascent of
MOUNT HAYDEN:
A New Chapter of Western Discovery

I was never fully satisfied with my explorations of the Upper Yellowstone region in 1870. What I then saw, and the discoveries made by Dr. Hayden's Geological Corps in 1871, begot in me the desire again to visit that Wonderland, with a view more fully to examine the surroundings of those particular localities which had so greatly excited the curiosity of the public. Our distress at the loss of a comrade, and the little time we had for extended observation and careful description of what we saw, convinced me that the half had not been seen or told of the freaks of nature in this secluded wilderness. One of the most remarkable as well as valuable discoveries—the Mammoth Hot Springs at Gardiner River—was reserved to be the grandest trophy of Dr. Hayden's Expedition. It was with the hope, therefore, that I might more fully comprehend what I had seen, and aid somewhat in the discovery of other wonders, that I concluded to avail myself of an invitation from Dr. Hayden to join his U. S. Geological Survey in July last, and accompany it in its visit to the National Park.

With a view to explore the country south of the Yellowstone, and especially in the immediate vicinity of Snake River,—of which so many, almost fabulous, stories had been told,—Dr. Hayden placed his assistant,

Captain James Stevenson, in charge of a part of his company, with instructions to approach the Park from that direction, while he, with the other members of the expedition, should proceed over the route of the previous year by way of Fort Ellis, up the Yellowstone River. Both parties were to meet in the Upper Geyser Basin of the Fire Hole River. This southern route had peculiar charms for me. It lay through a region practically unexplored, which must in a few years be penetrated by railroads and filled with people. It was now full of wild streams, vast lava beds, desolate sand tracts, mountain lakes, and long ranges of lofty mountains,—amid which the Snake River, true to its name, pursued its serpentine course to the Pacific, overlooked for hundreds of miles by the lofty range of Tetons, so long and widely known as the great landmarks of this part of the continent.

The company under Captain Stevenson's command had been several days at Fort Hall, in the Territory of Idaho, making preparation for their departure, before I joined it. I arrived at Ross's Fork, a station on the stage road from Utah to Montana, on the morning of our national anniversary. An ambulance which had been sent from Fort Hall for my use was in waiting, and I left almost immediately upon my arrival for that post. Lest the present Fort Hall should be mistaken for the old fur-trader's post of the same name, built by Nathaniel Wyeth as long ago as 1830, it is proper here to state that it is a new government fort, erected within the past three years, some forty miles distant from the ruins of the ancient post whose name it bears. Mount Putnam, named after the commandant of the fort, lifts its snow-crowned peak on the right to the height of 13,000 feet. Scarcely less conspicuous or majestic than the Tetons, appar-

Hen grouse in mountain dandelions.

Cow moose, Snake River.

ently a member of the same range, it gives dignity and grandeur to the landscape whose features it overlooks.

All our preparations being completed, the morning of the twelfth day of July was designated by Capt. Stevenson for our departure. Captain Putnam, to whom we had been under repeated obligations during our stay at the fort, afforded us all possible assistance. The boys were roused early, and the work of packing commenced. Great skill is required to perform this labor well and adroitly. Our packers were adepts in the art, and it was marvelous to witness with what precision and celerity they threw, looped, and fastened the lash-rope around the body of a pack-mule, by what is known as the "diamond hitch." The pack-saddle, when firmly secured to the back of a mule, bears no small resemblance to the common saw-buck of the street wood-sawyer, the four horns corresponding to the four upright projections of the cross pieces. Every part of it is made available for transportation. Tents, cooking utensils, clothing, engineering instruments, photographic apparatus, everything that enters into the outfit of any expedition through an unexplored region, is fastened to it with ropes, and the cincho, to which is attached the lash-rope, thrown around the whole. It would astonish any

ON THE MARCH

one who beheld the process for the first time, to see what immense loads may be packed upon the backs of horses and mules, in a compass sufficiently small to avoid serious collision with rocks and trees along the bridle-paths and trails through the forests and fastnesses of the mountains.

By ten o'clock our animals were packed and awaiting the order to start. The members of our party were each mounted on a strong horse, and as we passed out of the sally-port of the fort and descended into the valley, our appearance, to an eastern eye, would have been picturesque enough.

Bull elk sheds his velvet.

Facing page: Jackson Hole terrain from Signal Mountain.

Following pages: Dawn on a Snake River side channel.

We left Mr. Adams and Mr. Nicholson at Fort Hall; the former to follow us on the fifteenth and overtake us by hard riding,—the latter to take observations and determine the latitude and longitude of the Fort.

Moving on to Blackfoot Creek, a tributary of Snake River, we made an early camp.

Our train was in motion early the next morning, and we traveled leisurely over an arid and sandy plain, destitute of water. The heat towards mid-day became very oppressive, and our thirst intolerable. We had neglected taking a supply of water in our canteens, and until we reach Sandy Creek, a tributary of the Blackfoot, none could be obtained. Our animals suffered greatly, and towards the close of the day's journey were with difficulty urged forward. A fine greyhound, which had been presented to Capt. Stevenson by Capt. Putnam, fell from thirst and exhaustion and died upon the trail; and another would have suffered a like fate had not his master dug a hole through the sand into the damp clay and half-buried him in it, while a comrade rode at full speed to Sandy Creek and returned with water to relieve the suffering animal. Just before we reached Sandy Creek a light rain came on, and we caught a few drops in our rubber ponchos, which greatly invigorated us. Our poor animals, too, seemed to gather a new life as they felt the grateful moisture. I do not remember ever to have experienced the effects of thirst more than during this day's march. We made but fifteen miles advance, but the day was nearly spent when we went into camp.

Our camp at this place was in the midst of a miniature desert, and we left it as soon after daylight the

"Trap-rock" at Eagle Rock, now known as Idaho Falls.

next morning as possible. Pursuing our way through the sand, at noon we arrived at Eagle Rock Bridge, the point where the stage-road to Montana crosses Snake River. Here we see one of the remarkable features of this remarkable river,—its passage through an immense table of trap-rock, where it is narrowed from a width of four or five hundred yards to less than thirty, while its depth cannot be measured with a plumb and line. It is like a river set up on edge, and boils, whirls, and surges in its course like Niagara. The water is almost of an inky blackness, and seems to take its hue from the dark chasm through which it passes. The bridge is thrown across the narrowest place; and

though not greatly elevated above the water, such is the fury of the stream beneath it that one is very glad to feel that he has crossed it in safety. The same peculiarity which marks this locality may be seen on a much grander scale at the Dalles of the Columbia in Oregon, where that river has worked a channel of about one hundred feet in width and fifteen miles long through a table of trap-rock. Curious erosions have been wrought by the elements in the rocks in this vicinity. They are full of pot-holes and give a strange appearance to the immediate landscape. In many places where the rocks have been broken so as to divide the orifices, they are very jagged, and seem more like the work of man than nature.

On our arrival at Taylor's Bridge we were obliged, before going further, to determine whether we would follow up the main stream of Snake River or cross the country directly to the north of Henry's Fork. We had almost concluded upon the latter course when a trapper known as "Beaver Dick," who had just left the North Fork, informed us that we could ford the river above the Teton branch, but that the South Fork was impassable,—thus confirming our good judgment in selecting the route to the North Fork. Accordingly we renewed our march in the afternoon, and camped at a point five miles north of the Bridge.

Our route the next day was by the stage road to the station known as Market Lake. The marsh upon our left swarmed with mosquitoes, and the weather being very hot, we passed a tedious day. Tortured by these insects, our two burros stampeded with their packs and gave us a three-mile chase. The mail-coach came

Morning view from Deadman's Bar.

up soon after we encamped, bringing Mr. Adams, who had letters and papers for nearly all our boys.

This portion of Snake River valley was pretty thoroughly explored by Lieutenant Mullan in the winter of 1853–4. When he visited it, Market Lake, now a dry sandy depression in the prairie, was a large and beautiful sheet of water twelve or fourteen miles in length. He traveled along its margin for more than eight miles, and then diverged to Snake River. He was told by trappers and others that the lake had been formed but a few years: that before its formation its bed was an immense prairie bottom and the favorite resort for game of all kinds. The old mountaineers held it in high repute as a hunting-ground,—and whenever their provisions failed, always joined each other in an expedition to this favorite spot, which was known among them as "the market." "Let us go to market," was an invitation which was understood among trappers to indicate a desire to renew supplies from this every-bountiful resource. Captain Mullan gave it the name of Market Lake, to perpetuate what he at that time supposed was a legend connected with it;—but could he see the dry and arid plain which it presents to the eye today, all doubt of its early uses would be dispelled. A freak of the subterranean streams, not less strange and unaccountable than that which filled it and converted it into a magnificent lake, has now emptied it, and changed it into a forbidding desert.

We bade farewell to civilization at daylight on the morning of the 16th, and plunged into the rocky wilderness which lay between us and the North Fork. never before had this desolate clime echoed to the clatter of so large and gay a company. Thirty-seven mounted men and twenty-five pack animals could hardly fail to disturb the unbroken slumber of a region which, from every rock and tree and mountain, answers to the faintest sound with reduplicated murmurs. But as we looked before us and beheld, rising through the

Bull moose, Hedrick Pond.

Facing page: Marshland beaver dam.

morning vapors, the glinting sides and summits of the Tetons, we felt that even this country, desolate and virgin as it was, had a thrilling history. Those grand old mountains covered with eternal snow had, by their very isolation, pointed the way to the Pacific to all the early explorers, from the days of Lewis and Clarke, through the mountain passes and river mazes of this the most intricate part of the continent. Guided by them, Hunt in 1811 led his little half-starved band out of the almost inextricable wilderness of the Bighorn Mountains, and pursued his long and tortuous journey to the Columbia. Often did they serve during his years of wandering to guide Bonneville to the friendly wigwams of the Bannacks or Shoshones. And in the recent history of the country, the first sight of them has often assured the perplexed gold-hunter that he was on the right path to the Northern Eldorado. Rough, jagged, and pointed, they stood out before us nearer than I had ever before seen them, shining like gigantic crystals in the morning sunbeams. As I gazed upon the loftiest peak of the three, and followed up its steep and rock-ribbed sides to their acute summit, I tried to calculate the risks of our contemplated clamber, and communed with myself as to the possibility of its successful achievement. The outline of the mountain from this point of view presented so many concave reaches and precipitous ascents, that I began to regard as impossible the attainment of its top; and yet, as an achievement as well for the expansive and magnificent view to be obtained from it as for any renown it might give, it seemed to me to be worthy of the greatest risks and strongest efforts. Beaver Dick told

Teton Range from the south shore of Jackson Lake.

21

us, that though many times attempted, the ascent of the great Teton had never been accomplished. And this was the opinion of the Indians. Indeed, as late as the visit of Captain Reynolds to this region in 1860, the opinion was prevalent that the Tetons were surrounded by a tract of country so full of rocks and wild streams and perpetual snows as to be entirely inaccessible.

Mr. Hunt bestowed upon them the name of Pilot Knobs, because of the frequent benefit he derived from them as landmarks, though previous to his time they had received from the early French explorers the name they now bear of Tetons, from their similarity in form to the female breast. But 'tis distance that lends enchantment to such a view of these mountains, for when nearly approached, those beautiful curvilinear forms that obtained for them this delicate appellation become harsh and rugged and angular; and the comparison used by Professor Hayden, of "Shark's teeth," to represent their appearance, is more truthful and striking. The name is a misnomer, and if instead—as some insist is the case—they had been called the three Titans, it would have better illustrated their relation to the surrounding country.

Our course was through a treeless, desolate country of sand and rock, marked by few great inequalities of surface, and well calculated for railroad improvement. After

The Cathedral Group, through Cunningham cabin.

Facing page: Lightning on the banks of the Snake.

The Grand Teton from Pine Creek Pass, Idaho.

traveling seventeen miles we reached the North, or Henry's Fork of Snake River, so named after the first fur-trader who crossed the Rocky Mountains and established himself in this country.

We camped near the base of two high buttes, whose peculiar formation excited our curiosity. With every external appearance of basalt, they were as soft and friable as sandstone. An impromptu party, of which the writer was one, left camp for the purpose of exploring these singular Knobs. Ascending the most northerly of the two to the height of nearly a thousand feet, they quite unexpectedly found themselves standing upon the igneous rim,

Bison in morning mists.

not more than fifty feet in width, of an enormous crater, whose yawning depth of three hundred feet, and widely extended jaws of a thousand feet or more, left no doubt as to the original character of the mountain. It was an extinct volcano. The rim of the crater, broken in the direction of our camp, denoted the course of the lava, and our geologist gave as a reason for its resemblance to sand-rock, that the overflow had occurred under water, which produced disintegration, and the particles on reuniting formed a volcanic sand-

stone. From the extreme rareness of its occurrence, this discovery, next to that of the "Quebec Group," was deemed the most important of the expedition. We descended at an angle of about 45° into the crater, the bottom of which was covered with sage-brush and bunch-grass.

Looking up from this interior at the rim, its various erosions, fissures, and inequalities of blackened masses presented a most grotesque appearance. Externally the lava on the mountain sides assumes a great variety

Bull elk in velvet.

of fantastic forms, prominent among which are those of numerous ovens with lofty chimneys, interspersed among turrets, castles, spires, keeps, and towers. The view from the rim commands a vast extent of country. On the south we behold the valley of the great Snake River, blackened with the huge and shapeless masses of basalt scattered over it, and the doublings and twistings of the mighty river itself as it struggles with a thousand impediments on its sinuous course to the Pacific. Eastward, Henry's Fork and its tributaries emerge into view from the mountains and hasten across the plain to their union with the Snake, while all around us the distant horizon is decked with isolated peaks and interminable ridges.

Among the strangely fretted rocks near the base of this volcano, was one which Mr. Adams called "Kenilworth Castle," from the resemblance it bore to that ruin. Upon that portion of it corresponding to the banqueting hall, we found an Indian inscription, which doubtless was intended to perpetuate incidents in the life of some successful hunter. As the rock was soft, the inscription could not have been very ancient. It represented buffalo-hunts, encounters with the grizzly, slaying of deer, elk, and moose,—cranes, mounted hunters and hunters on foot, all sufficiently accurate for identification. I have seen upon the elk and buffalo robes of the Blackfeet many inscriptions of like character; and with that nation more perhaps than any other, it is a custom by some means to perpetuate the memory of their great chiefs, and great events in their history. I conclude from the fact that the Blackfeet, within the past half century, were the

Facing page: Storm over the Tetons, viewed from the Triangle X Ranch.

most warlike tribe in the vicinity of this inscription, that it was the work of one of their famous hunters.

Among our own hunters was a trapper named Shep Medary—a lively, roystering mountaineer, who liked nothing better than to get a joke upon any unfortunate "pilgrim" or "tender foot" who was verdant enough to confide in his stories of mountain life.

"What a night!" said Shep, as the moon rose broad and clear—"what a glorious night for drivin' snipe!"

Here was something new. Two of our young men were eager to learn all about the mystery.

"Driving snipe! what's that, Shep! Tell us about it."

"Did ye never hear?" replied Shep, with a face expressive of wonder at their ignorance. "Why, it's as old as the mountains, I guess; we always choose such weather as this for drivin' snipe. The snipe are fat now, and they drive better, and they're better eatin' too. I tell you, a breakfast of snipe, broiled on the buffalo chips, is not bad to take, is it, Dick?"

Beaver Dick, who had just arrived in camp, thus appealed to, growled an assent to the proposition contained in Shep's question; and the boys, more anxious than ever, pressed Shep for an explanation.

"Maybe," said one of them, "maybe we can drive the snipe tonight and get a mess for breakfast: what have we got to do, Shep?"

"Oh well," responded Shep, "if you're so plaguey ignorant, I'm afear'd you won't do. Howsomever, you can try. You boys get a couple of them gunny-sacks and candles, and well go out and start 'em up."

Elated with the idea of having a mess of snipe for breakfast, the two young men, under Shep's direction,

Near the Oxbow Bend of the Snake.

THE SNIPE HUNT

"Now," said Shep, stationing the the boys about ten feet apart, "open your sacks, be sure and keep the mouths of 'em wide open, and after we leave, light your candles and hold 'em well into the sack, so that the snipe can see, and the rest of us will drive 'em up. It may take a little spell to get 'em started, but if you wait patiently they'll come."

With this assurance the snipe drivers left them and returned immediately to camp.

"I've got a couple of green 'uns out there," said he with a sly wink. "They'll wait some time for the snipe to come up, I reckon."

The boys followed directions,—the sacks were held wide open, the candles kept in place. There they stood, the easy prey of the remorseless mosquitoes. An hour passed away, and yet from the ridge above the camp the light of the candles could be seen across the plain. Shep now stole quietly out of camp, and, making a long circuit, came up behind the victims and, raising a war-whoop, fired his pistol in the air.

The boys dropped their sacks and started on a two-forty pace for camp, coming in amid the laughter and shouts of their companions.

Beaver Dick pitched his "wakiup" near our camp, and, with his Indian wife and half-breed children, added a novel feature to the company. Dick is quite a character, and during the time he spent with us displayed personal traits that would make him a fitting hero for a popular dime-novel. He is an Englishman, has been engaged in trapping for twenty-one years, is perfectly familiar with all the accessible portions of the Rocky Mountains, and has adopted many of the habits

each equipped with a gunny-sack and candle, followed him out upon the plain, half a mile from camp, accompanied by some half-dozen members of our party. The spot was chosen because of its proximity to a marsh which was supposed to be filled with snipe. In reality it was the swarming-place for mosquitoes.

Facing page: Arrowleaf balsamroot, Jackson Lake, Mt. Woodring, and Mt. Moran.

and pursuits of the Indians. He, however, has made it a point twice a year to visit some civilized region in order to dispose of his furs and obtain supplies. We must depend upon his guidance in fording streams, crossing mountain passes, and avoiding collision with unfriendly tribes. His children are already great favorites with our company, and his dusky wife seems a quiet, inoffensive creature, whose highest ambition is to learn how best to serve her lord and master.

Under his guidance, we broke camp at early dawn and followed up the valley of Henry's Fork, which we crossed in safety at the ford. The task was not accomplished without difficulty, as the bank of the stream where we entered it was very abrupt and the current very rapid. It required great care to prevent the smaller pack-animals from being swept away. The water in the channel mounted nearly to their backs. A dog belonging to one of the company was carried yelping down the stream, out of sight, and we supposed it was lost. It made its appearance in camp two hours afterwards, sadly humiliated by the adventure. The stream was full of the large salmon-trout peculiar to all streams flowing into the Pacific; several that we caught weighed from two to three pounds each. In form and appearance these beautiful fish resemble the brook-trout, but they are very much larger, and, except in single instances, the spots upon them are brown instead of crimson. The flesh is a rich salmon color, and extremely delicate. If cleaned and cooked while fresh from the water, they furnish a delicious meal.

Among our riding-horses was a little cream-colored cayuse, which after fording the stream, performed the extraordinary feat of bucking completely out of his saddle while it was fastened upon him by cincho and breast-strap.

BEAVER DICK AND HIS FAMILY

The poor fellow who mounts a bucking cayuse without knowing how to manage it, is very sure to be thrown over its head or slipped over its haunches, at the infinite risk of breaking his neck or being kicked to death. But with a man on its back who knows how to avoid these calamities, there is something ludicrous in the wrathful leaps and vicious dodges of the animal.

The little ponies, which take their name from the Cayuse Indians, possess, as a native quality, this habit of bucking, or jumping high in air as we have seen lambs do, striking, with every joint stiffened, all four feet forcibly upon the earth. The concussion is so violent that, unless the rider is experienced, one or two efforts will be enough to dash him to the ground. The very appearance of the animal is frightful. The ears are thrown back close to its head, the eyes put on a vicious expression, it froths at the mouth, seizes the bit with its teeth, tries to bite, and in every possible manner evinces the utmost enmity for its rider. Bucking is deemed as incurable as balking—whip and spur and kind treatment being alike in vain.

Mr. Adams left the camp the morning after our arrival, in company with Shep Medary, on a hurried return to Fort Hall, to procure more pack animals, and recruit our waning stock of supplies. Growing in great profusion all around our camp, we were delighted to find those articles of food so much prized by the Indians—the camas and yamph roots. The camas is both flour and potatoes for several wandering nations; and it is found in the most barren and desolate regions in greatest quantity. The camas is a small round root, not unlike an onion in appearance. It is sweet to the

"If cleaned and cooked while fresh from the water, they furnish a delicious meal."

33

The Teton Range from Bridger-Teton National Forest: (from left) Nez Perce Peak, South Teton, Middle Teton, Grand Teton, Mt. Owen.

taste, full of gluten, and very satisfying to a hungry man. The Indians have a mode of preparing it which makes it very relishable. In a hole of a foot in depth, and six feet in diameter, from which the turf has been carefully removed, they build a fire for the purpose of heating the exposed earth-surface, while in another fire, at the same time, they heat a sufficient number of flat rocks to serve as a cover. After the heating process is completed the roots are spread over the bottom of the hole, covered with the turf, the heated rocks spread above, a fire built upon them, and the process of cooking produces about the same change in the camas that is produced by roasting in coffee. It also preserves it in a suitable form for ready use.

The yamph is a longer and smaller bulb than the camas, not quite as nutritious, and eaten raw. Either of these roots contains nutriment sufficient to support life; and often, in the experience of the tribes of the mountains, winters have been passed with no other food. There is a poison camas, which is sometimes mistaken for the genuine root, that cannot be eaten without fatal results. It always grows where the true camas is found, and much care is necessary to avoid missing the two while gathering in any quantity. So great is the esteem in which the camas is held, that many of the important localities of this country are names after it.

The great theme of talk about out campfire was the proposed ascent of the Tetons. Beaver Dick said our design was not new. The ascent had been often tried, and always without success. An old trapper by the name of Michaud, as long ago as 1843, provided himself with ropes, rope ladders, and other aids, and spent days

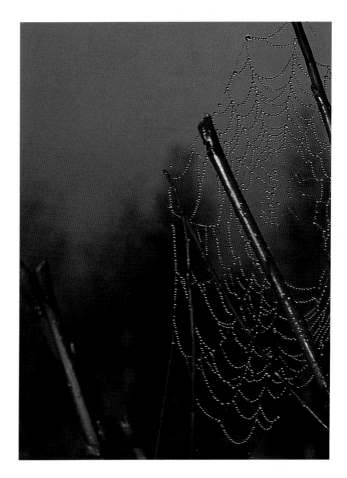

in the effort, but met with so many obstructions he finally gave it up in despair. "You can try," said Dick, significantly; "but you'll wind up in the same way."

After a ride of ten miles, we arrived at mid-day at the Middle Fork of the Snake, or the Mad river of Mr. Hunt. It is not as large as the North Fork, but much more rapid. All day the Tetons reared their heads in full view. From the summit, midway to the base, they seemed to be covered with perpetual snow. In the buttressed sides, as the eye scanned them critically, many places were seen where the rocks were nearly vertical and which it would be impossible to scale. They were apparently intrenched in a wilderness of rocks, as inaccessible as their summits.

Our camp, the next day, was thirteen miles nearer the Tetons, which assumed a loftier appearance and seemed more distant than ever.

Fireweed and mule deer.

Facing page: Snake River at the Buffalo Fork.

We followed up Conant's Creek another day over high, rolling ridges and through deep coulées, which were filled with groves of small poplars. These thickets afforded fine retreats and shelter from the weather for elk, deer, and bear, though our hunter, who came in empty at night, complained bitterly that the country is destitute of game. Looking at the mountain ridge, near the source of Middle Fork, a depression there suggested the practicability of a railroad from Snake River to the Geysers.

On the following day we pushed forward to the Big Cottonwood, a stream fed by the melting of the snow in the gorges of the mountains. Its banks were full, and the stream was a perfect torrent. Beaver Dick told us that it is generally dry from the point where we are camped to its mouth at this season. These snow streams in the mountains are very common, and in mining countries they often afford the only means of developing the richest gold placers.

Just below our camp we found a patch of strawberries, a luxury

"Our hunter killed an antelope, and we feasted upon fresh steaks."

Facing page: "Moose Crossing": Oxbox Bend of the Snake.

which none appreciate more highly than those who have been living upon canned fruits and bacon. The rich bunch-grass in the bottoms and foot-hills contrasted strangely with the rock pasture we left hind us. We seemed to have entered a region of plenty. Our hunter killed an antelope, and we feasted upon fresh steaks. But we made slow progress, on account of the great number of badger and prairie-dog holes.

Eight miles of difficult travel took us fairly into the Teton basin. This basin, hid away among the mountains, is like an oasis in the desert. It embraces an area of about eight hundred square miles, and is carpeted with the heaviest and largest bunch-grass I have every seen. It is bounded on three sides by a range of snow-capped mountains, and forms a complete *cul-de-sac*. Camas and yamph grow all over it in great abundance, and in the lowlands and along the streams are found large patches of strawberries of the finest flavor. Our entrance into this valley was effected by traveling over high table-lands and rolling foot-hills, which for a distance of twelve or fifteen miles were covered with vegetation. Innumerable crystal streams flow from the surrounding mountains into the Teton river, which traverses the valley longitudinally.

All the resources of our camp were now put in requisition to favor the ascent of the Great Teton. Mr. Adams, who had returned to Fort Hall from North Fork, was daily expected. He was to bring with him barometric instruments necessary to determine the altitude of the lofty peaks. Mr. Stevenson and the writer concluded to occupy the time until he should

arrive in a preliminary reconnaissance of the mountains. Accordingly, on the morning of the 24th of July after an early breakfast, we mounted our horses and proceeded up the cañon above our camp. Following the main stream, we passed in the distance of three miles thirty or forty beautiful cascades. For that entire distance the walls of the cañon seemed full for their reverberations. Many of them were fashioned by the descent of lateral streams into the main Teton, and followed each other in almost continuous succession down the rocks. Their noisy laughter (we could not call it roar) was the only sound that broke the silence of the chasm through which we were passing. On every hand we

saw them through the pines, at a height of thousands of feet, veiling the rocks and leaping into pools of foamy whiteness.

There was no trail up the cañon, and we were obliged, as best we might, to pick our way over fallen trunks, through narrow ravines, and amid innumerable rocks. On our right the massive walls of fossiliferous limestone, nearly vertical, towered three thou-

sand feet above us. Looking up, we could see, at that amazing height, huge projections of shelving rock just over our heads, and lofty towers rising above them into the clear blue atmosphere. A feeling of dread, lest some of these mighty masses should be loosed and hurled upon us, was mingled with those sublimer emotions which this spectacle evoked.

While we were riding carelessly along, a black bear rushed from behind a rock and ran on before us. We gave it instant chase, but the ground being covered with bowlders, it soon distanced us, and coming to a tree which had fallen across the stream, it ran across the trunk to the opposite side. In attempting to ford the stream in pursuit, the rapidity of the current nearly swept my horse from his feet. He was swung around among the bowlders, and in extricating himself tore a shoe from his foot. A second effort enabled me to reach the other side, but Bruin meantime, had escaped.

In traveling the distance of ten miles from our camp, we had accomplished an ascent of two thousand

"…but Bruin meantime, had escaped."

feet, when we struck the line of snow. Our horses were tired out, and the ravine up which we had advanced was now so full of rocks and bowlders as to render further progress on horseback impossible.

We lariated our horses, and proceeded to clamber over the immense granite bowlders that jutted from the side of the chasm. The frequent scratches and ridges apparent upon the surface of the larger rocks bore incontestable evidence that in the long ago some mighty glacier had pushed its way through opposing mountains, and left this long ravine to mark its track to the valley. Above the granite and overlying it, we found a stratum of gray sandstone, fragments of which were scattered over the sides of the ravine. Still above this was a superincumbent mass of lava, several hundred feet in thickness.

Following in the direction of the Tetons, which were hidden by intercepting rocks, after three hours' scrambling over yawning precipices, immense bowlders and vast snow-fields, we stood upon the summit of the ridge, at an elevation of 10,500 feet above ocean level. Expecting here to find ourselves upon a plateau which stretched to the base of the mountains, what was our disappointment at beholding, between us and it, an immense gorge with perpendicular sides, two thousand feet deep, and more than three thousand feet in width. A field of snow of measureless depth concealed the bottom of the chasm, and the hollow murmur of a creek which struck our ears seemed to come from the center of the earth. It must have been at least twelve hundred feet beneath the surface of the snow. On the right, in the midst of

View from Signal Mountain, clouds intervening.

"Lake Moran," now known as Snowdrift Lake. Photo by Tony Huhn

the snow-field, was a large lake of marvelous beauty. Upon its dark blue bosom swans and other aquatic fowl were sporting. We named this sheet of water Lake Cowan, in honor of Hon. B. R. Cowan, Assistant Secretary of the Interior. It is located in that portion of the Teton range known among the early trappers as Jackson's Hole.

From our point of observation we discovered a small lake, lying at the base of the Tetons, the surface of which as covered with ice and snow. The perspiration occasioned by the severe exercise we had taken soon disappeared before the chill blasts from the mountains, and we found it necessary to shelter ourselves beneath some friendly rocks, whence we made a critical examination of the Great Teton, and the slopes ascending to the ridge or plateau which isolates those three peaks from all surrounding mountains. This immense bench, though not

divided by erosions, seems at some former time to have been the base of one enormous mountain, the summit of which, by time and the elements, has been divided into the three Teton peaks. The view from where I stood was unlike any other I had ever beheld; in all the elements of savage grandeur, I doubt if it

could be surpassed. Rocks and snow, with a few patches of trees, composed the entire scenery; but these were arranged in such fantastic forms and on so unlimited a scale as to defy all effort at description. It was bewildering—overpowering—but needed something beautiful, something upon which the eye could rest pleasurably, to relieve the stern lineaments everywhere revealed.

The ascent of the Great Teton, to look at the lofty peak of rugged granite, seemed impossible. On either side, the angle at which it rose was apparently a continuous precipice from top to bottom. Even to clamber up the plateau to its base was a labor full of difficulty. After crossing the glacier in the chasm beneath us, we would have to select a pathway up the plateau between the confronting ridges which everywhere swelled from its irregular sides, and crept in tortuous protuberances to its very summit. A mistake in the selection would be fatal to success, and we would be compelled to return and commerce anew, for we could not cross laterally from one to another of these walled ravines. Two hours of observation, if they failed to exalt, did not dampen our courage, and we returned to our horses more determined than ever that the enterprise should not fail for want of effort. We selected a spot for a temporary camp, at the first grass we met with while descending the cañon, intending from that point to accomplish the ascent and return in a single day. Night was now approaching, and we hastened towards the camp.

When within three miles of it, we came upon our fearless topographers, Mr. Beckler, who, with a shotgun loaded with small shot, stood face to face with a she grizzly and two cubs, which he had frightened from their lair in the thicket, while in search of small game. Fortunately, in attempting to discharge his gun it missed fire, and probably saved him from a deadly encounter with the irritated animal, or a hasty ascent of a tree as a possible alternative. We prevailed upon him to return with us, and await a more favorable opportunity for a tussle with grizzlies.

During our absence two of the boys had felled a tall pine that stood upon the bank of the stream for a foot-bridge, and while trimming off the branches from the prostrate trunk, contrived to lose the axe in the river, about forty-five feet from the shore. It was the only one remaining in camp, two others having been broken. We could hardly have lost anything so constantly in demand, or so difficult to replace. It had sunk, and in the clear stream lay in full view on the bottom of the river, in the midst of the rapids. The boys had made every effort they could devise to recover it, but in vain, and it was given up as lost. Two

Trumpeter swan.

Facing page: The Cathedral Group.

other members of our party had killed and brought into camp a good-sized black bear, which is one of the most formidable animals in the Rocky Mountains. We were made aware, by the finding of a flint arrowhead, of the fact that our present camp had, in days gone by, been occupied by Indians. As long ago as the visit of Lewis and Clarke to this country, the Indian tribes had substituted sheet-iron for flint in the manufacture of their arrow-heads,—the material being supplied to them by the Hudson's Bay Company. Lewis and Clarke, on one occasion, bought several horses with a worn-out joint of stove-pipe. Judging from its appearance, many years must have elapsed since the arrow-head found by us was last in use; so this region, new to us, was long ago the occasional abode of the Indians.

Our party, while awaiting the arrival of Mr. Adams, spent the time in making various scientific observations. The three Tetons were found to be thirty miles east of the location assigned to them by all former geographers, and instead of being in Idaho, as generally supposed, were about a mile inside the western boundary of Wyoming.

Mr. Adams, accompanied by Dr. Curtis, the microscopist of the expedition, Shep Medary, guide, and two cavalrymen came into camp on the 26th of July. They had trailed our party from Fort Hall, a distance of 130 miles, in four days. A letter received from Dr. Hayden, announced the sudden death of Mrs. Blackmore, the estimable wife of Mr. William Blackmore. This melancholy event occurred at Bozeman, a few days after the arrival of Dr. Hayden's party, of which Mr. and Mrs. Blackmore were members, at that place.

The necessity for making the effort to obtain our axe is the only excuse that can be offered for incurring the risk it involved. But, without the axe, the company were in a condition of helplessness entirely irreparable. The depth of water where it lay was not more than three feet, but it was the very middle of the

Beaver-felled cottonwood

stream, which was one continuous torrent, and of icy temperature. An attempt made by one of the herders to reach the spot, by riding a horse into the stream, resulted in failure,—the current being too swift for even a horse to maintain his footing among the bowlders.

The member of the party who determined to recover it, accompanied by several of his comrades, proceeded to the spot, when, after removing all his clothing except his wrapper, a pair of woolen socks, and a silken handkerchief about his neck, he fastened around his chest a strong rope, the other end of which was passed around a tree which stood upon the bank in a bend of the stream about seventy feet above, and was then intrusted to the stout hands of the wagon-master. The uproar of the water would render verbal communication impossible, from the moment he entered the stream; so signals were agreed upon, by which the men on shore could understand his wishes. The bottom of the river was composed of smooth cobblestones and slippery bowlders,—a most uncertain footing.

Thus prepared, he stepped into the torrent, which every instant threatened to whirl him off his feet. Holding firmly by the rope, his feet braced against the current, his body inclined at an angle of forty-five degrees, he waded sidewise by slow steps, to the spot where the axe was lying. Reaching down to grasp it, he was unable to resist the force of the current by which his arm was impelled below it. Obeying his signal, his comrades drew upon the rope and enabled him to gain a position above the axe. Here he found that in order to reach it, his body must necessarily be submerged, and a loss of footing might be attended with serious conse-

North face of the Grand through lodgepole pines.

RESCUING THE AXE

quences. A plunge was made, but the current still swept his arm beyond the axe. A second effort was attended with a like result. At the third plunge he succeeded in firmly grasping the handle. As he raised it the force of the current against the broad side of the blade turned his body partially around, and in attempting to regain his position he lost his foothold, and was whirled in among the bowlders. The rope, drawing over one shoulder diagonally to the shore forced his head under the water and held it there. Thus extended in the stream, it was impossible to recover an upright position against the powerful rapid,—and he was rolled over and over upon and amid the rocks and bowlders, sometimes above, and sometimes beneath the maddened water, until by the sheer force of the current he was literally driven to the shore, covered with severe bruises and contusions, and nearly exhausted.

As he neared the bank, suffering intensely for want of breath, he made one more determined effort to regain his feet, and, securing a temporary foothold, succeeded in raising his head for an instant above the surface, when he heard from one of his comrades on shore the exclamation, "Well we've seen the last of *that* axe." The next instant he was again swept among the bowlders;—but as he rolled over and the waters closed above him, he raised the axe above the surface of the stream, in full view of his comrades, in mute testimony of the triumph he could in no other manner express. The current was sufficiently strong to sweep from his feet the pair of woolen socks, and untie a hard knot in the handkerchief around his neck. All unpleasant

Facing page: Cottonwood Creek.

consequences of the undertaking soon yielded to proper treatment.

On returning to camp, I was invited to dine with "Beaver Dick," who had cooked a beaver in the mountain style, and wished to demonstrate its superiority to the ordinary methods of preparing game for the table. I confess that my appetite was not much sharpened, on being told that the animal had been boiled entire, and that the dressing was all done after the cooking was completed; but the superior flavor of the meat, its

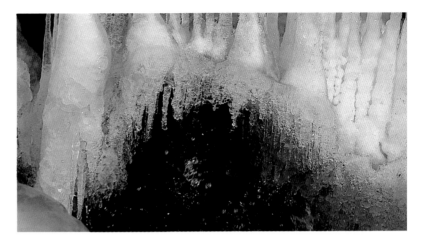

succulence and tenderness, convinced me that, squeamishness aside, beaver was all the better for being cooked according to the civilized method of cooking pigeons.

Mr. Jackson, our persevering photographic artist, took a great number of views of the scenery in this vicinity—including many of the cascades in the Cañon, and the Tetons from all points of the compass. He is an indefatigable worker, and as often camps alone in some of the wild glens as with the company. Give him fine scenery, and he forgets danger and difficulty in the effort to "get a negative."

Our ascending party, fourteen in number, being fully organized, we left camp at 10 o'clock, on the morning of the 28th July, and followed up the cañon nine miles, to the spot chosen for our temporary camp. Here we rested, and dined; after which Messrs. Adams and Taggart ascended a mountain on the left of the camp to a plateau 3,000 feet above it, from which

they were able to determine the general features of the route to the base of the Great Teton. That peak rose majestically in the distance above a hundred smaller peaks, its sharp sides flecked with snow, and its bold gray summit half buried in fleecy clouds. It was indeed the lord of the empyrean. Pressing on toward it, they ascended a point of the plateau separated by an intervening chasm of nearly a thousand feet in depth from the elevation over which their pathway lay. The setting sum admonished them that they had barely time to return to camp before dark. They reached there in time to join the boys in a game of snow-balling, a singular amusement for the last days of July.

At half past four the next morning, the thermometer being 11° above zero, the party was aroused, and after partaking of a hearty breakfast, each man provided with an alpine staff, and a bacon sandwich for mid-day lunch, departed from camp, intent upon reaching the topmost summit of the loftiest Teton. The

Facing page: The view from the west: (from left) Storm Point and Cascade Canyon, Mt. Owen, Gunshot Notch, Grand Teton, Lake Solitude in foreground.

PHOTOGRAPHING IN HIGH PLACES

had ascended, and took in an immense view of the surrounding country. Far as the eye could reach, looking northward, peak rose above peak, and range stretched beyond range, all glistening in the sunbeams like solid crystal. In the immediate vicinity of our position, the eye roamed over vast snow-fields, rocky chasms, straggling pine forests, and countless cascades.

The snow-field over which we next traveled, instead of the smoothness of a freshly-covered plain, was as irregular, as full of hummocks and billows as the rocks beneath it and the storms which for years had swept over it could possibly make it. It presented the appearance of an ocean frozen when the storm was at its height. Clambering over the first ridge, we traveled on in the direction of the second, which obstructed our view of the Tetons. Our route was over huge bowlders alternated with snow, and at this hour of the morning, before the sun had visited it, no traveling could be more unpleasant. We found our alpenstocks of infinite service, and we may thank them for the many falls we escaped upon the slippery surface, as well as for the comparative safety of many we made. Two miles of this kind of exercise brought us to the second ridge, which was composed of crumbling rock, and at least six hundred feet above the level of the field we had passed over. The view from this point

first two miles of the journey lay directly up the cañon, and over countless heaps of fallen trees. This tedious course of travel only terminated to give place to another, still more wearisome, through a ravine, and up a steep acclivity which we were enabled only to ascend by clinging to the points and angles of projecting rocks. Pausing at the summit to take breath, we saw lying between us and the first icy ridge a vast field of snow. Our aneroids showed that we were 9,000 feet above the ocean level—a height which entirely overlooked the walls of the cañon we

Cunningham cabin (built in 1890).

Cow elk amid lodgepole pines.

was magnificent, but almost disheartening, from the increasing obstruction it presented to our progress. Another stretch of snow, rising to a sharp ridge, lay in front of us, at least five miles in length, across which, in our line of travel, was another upheaval of crumbling rock. On our right, a thousand feet below, was the open, blue Lake Cowan.

Resuming labor, some of our party crawled around the side of the gorge, preferring rather to cross over the snowy ridge on our left, than to descent the slippery side of the elevation upon which we stood. Several projecting ledges of crumbling rock lay between them and the snow, from which, as they passed over them, detached masses rolled down the bank endangering the lives of all below. Mr. Beckler, by a sudden jump, barely escaped being crushed by a large rock, which whistled by him like an avalanche. As he jumped he fell, and rolled down upon an out-cropping bowlder, receiving an injury which disabled him. Others of the party slid down the ridge unharmed,

Lake Solitude (under ice) and Cascade Creek.

and encountered fewer difficulties in their journey along its base than its sides. The snow in the long ridge was at least two hundred and fifty feet in depth, and apparently as solid as the granite it covered. After a walk of more than a mile upon its glassy surface, we made a long descent to the right, and passed over a

Clouds clearing from Valhalla and Cascade canyons.

lake about 600 yards long by 200 wide, covered with ice from twelve to fifteen feet thick. There was nothing about this frozen water to indicate that it had ever been open. The ice which bound it, as well as the snow surrounding, seemed eternal. So pure and clear was this frozen surface, that one could see, even at its greatest thickness, the water gurgling beneath. At the distance from which we first saw it, we supposed this lake lay at the very base of the Tetons, but after we passed over it, there still stretched between us and that point two miles of cor-

rugated snow. Still receding and receding, those lofty peaks seemed to move before us like the Israelites' pillar of cloud, and had we not seen this last snow-field actually creeping up to the top, and into the recesses of that lofty crest, from which the peaks shoot upward to the heavens, we should most willingly have turned our faces campward from the present point of vision, and written over the whole expedition, "Impossible."

There is no greater wonder in mountain scenery on this continent, than the tendency it has to shorten distance to the eye and lengthen it to the feet. A range of

mountains apparently ten miles distant may be fifty miles away. A plain, to all appearances as smooth as a floor, is often broken into deep ravines, yawning chasms, and formidable foot-hills. Everything in distance and surface is deceptive.

Beyond the lake we ascended the last rocky ridge, more precipitous than the others, to take a last look at the dreary landscape.

We seemed to be in the midst of an arctic region. All around was snow and rock and ice. Forward or backward everything was alike bleak, barren and inhospitable; but our great labor was still unperformed. Encouraged by the certainty that we were upon the last of those great snow environments which lay at the feet of the mountains, we pushed onward to the base of the immense saddle between them. At this point several of the party, worn out with the day's exertions, and despairing of reaching the lofty summit which still towered five thousand feet in mockery above them, abandoned all further effort. Our kind surgeon, Dr. Reagles, had considerately accompanied us to the base of the

Clark's nutcracker and Mt. Wister.

ridge, provided with instruments and bandages in case of accident.

We lost no time in selecting from the numerous ravines that were made by the erosion of the friable rock from between the ascending granite ledges, such an one as we believed might be traversed to the top of the ridge without meeting lateral obstructions. Some of our party, mistaken in this, encountered when mid-way up the side a precipitous wall of granite, which made their return imperative. Five only of the company, after clambering over a snow-slide a thousand feet or more in width, reached the depression on the right of the Grand Teton which we called "The Saddle." The ascent thus far had tested the endurance of all who made it. It was only difficult or dangerous to those who had selected the wrong passage through the ledges. We ate part of our luncheon while upon "The Saddle," which we reached about noon, and rested there a quarter of an hour beneath the shadow of the Great Teton. It seemed, as we looked up its erect sides, to challenge us to attempt is ascent. As we gazed upon the glaciers, the concavities, the precipices which now in more formidable aspect than ever presented themselves to us, we were almost ready to admit that the task we had undertaken was impossible to perform. The mountain side, from the Saddle to the summit of the Grand Teton, arose at an angle of sixty degrees; broken by innumerable cavities and precipices.

Our leader, Captain Stevenson, had pushed on ahead, and when Messrs. Hamp, Spencer and the writer had reached "The Saddle," he was far up the mountain, lost to view in its intricacies. Our fears con-

The view from Glacier View Turnout.

cerning him were allayed by occasionally seeing his footprints in the debris. Very soon after we commenced the ascent, we found ourselves clambering around projecting ledges of perpendicular rocks, inserting our fingers into crevices so far beyond us that we reached them with difficulty, and poising our weight upon shelves not exceeding two inches in width, jutting from the precipitous walls of gorges from fifty to three hundred feet in depth. This toilsome process, which severely tested our nerves, was occasionally interrupted by large banks of snow, which had lodged upon some of the projections or in the concavities of the mountain side, — in passing over the yielding surface of which we obtained tolerable foothold, unless, as was often the case, there was a groundwork of ice beneath. When this occurred, we found the climbing difficult and hazardous. In many places, the water from the melting snow had trickled through it, and congealed the lower surface. This, melting in turn, had worn long openings between the ice and the mountain side, from two to four feet in width, down which we could look two hundred feet or more. Great care was necessary to avoid slipping into these crevices. An occasional spur of rock or ice, connecting the ice-wall with the mountain, was all that held these patches of snow in their places. In Europe they would have been called glaciers. Distrustful as we all were of their permanency, we were taught, before our toil was ended, to wish there had been more of them. As a general thing, they were more easi-

Moose and moon, Jackson Hole.

Facing page: "Mt. Hayden" from the summit of Middle Teton.

Sunset from Spread Creek.

MOUNT HAYDEN AND MOUNT MORAN — FROM THE WEST

ly surmounted than the bare rock precipices, though on one occasion they came near proving fatal to one of our party.

Mr. Hamp, fresh from his home in England, knew little of the properties of snow and ice, and at one of the critical points in our ascent, trusting too much to their support, slipped and fell. For a moment his destruction seemed inevitable, but with admirable dexterity he threw himself astride the icy ridge projecting from the mountain. Impelled by this movement, with one leg dangling in the crevice next the mountain side, and the other sweeping the snow outside the glacier, he slid with fearful rapidity, at an angle of forty-five degrees, for the distance of fifty feet, falling headlong into a huge pile of soft snow, which prevented his descent of a thousand feet or more down the precipitous side of the mountain. I saw him fall, and supposed he would be dashed to pieces. A moment afterwards he crawled from the friendly snow-heap and rejoined us unharmed, and we all united in a round of laughter, as thankful as it was hearty. This did not quiet that tremulousness of the nerves, of which extreme and sudden danger is so frequent a cause, and underlying our joy there was still a feeling of terror which we could not shake off. Pressing carefully forward, we attained a recess in the rocks, six hundred feet below the summit, where we halted.

While resting here, far above us, we heard the loud shouts of Captain Stevenson, which we answered. Soon he joined us, with the information that he had been arrested in his ascent, at a point two hundred feet above us, by an intervening rock, just too high for

*Bull elk bugling
beneath Falling Ice
Glacier, Mt. Moran.*

him to scale. It was perpendicular, and surmounted by a wide sheet of ice stretching upward towards the summit, and covered with snow. He had made several ineffectual efforts to reach the overhanging edge of the rock, and at one time lost his foothold, his entire weight coming upon his hands while he hung with his face to the wall. It was impossible without a leap to reach a standing place, and by loosening his hold without one he would drop several hundred feet down the mountain. Fortunately, there was a coating of ice and snow, which reached midway from his feet to his arms, and into this, by repeated kicks with the toe of his boot, he worked an indentation that afforded a poise for one foot. This enabled him to spring on one side to a narrow bench of rock, where he was safe.

We had periled life and limb to little purpose, if the small matter of five hundred feet was to prevent the accomplishment of our task. We determined, therefore, to ascend with Captain Stevenson and make another effort to scale the rock. When I saw the perilous position from which he had escaped, I could not but regard his preservation as almost miraculous. In spite of nervous exhaustion, Mr. Hamp had persevered in the attempt to climb the mountain, but as all upward progress from this point was extremely hazardous, he and Mr. Spencer were persuaded to avail themselves of a foot-hold in the rocks, while Captain Stevenson and I made a last essay to reach the pinnacle.

A rope which I had brought with me, cast over a slight projection above our heads, enabled me to draw myself up so as to fix my hands in a crevice of the rock,

and then, with my feet resting on the shoulders of Captain Stevenson, I easily clambered to the top. Letting the rope down to Captain Stevenson, he grasped it firmly, and by the aid of his staff soon worked his way to my side. The shelving expanse of ice overlying the rocky surface at an angle of 70°, and fastened to it by slight arms of the same brittle material, now presented an obstacle apparently insurmountable. Beside the danger of incurring a slide which would insure a rapid descent to the base of the mountain, there was the other risk, that the frail fastenings which held the ice-sheet to the rocks might give way while we were crawling over it, and the whole field be carried with us down the terrible precipice. But the top was just before us, not three hundred feet away, and we preferred the risk to an abandonment of the task. Laying hold of the rocky points at the side of the ice-sheet, we broke with our feet in its surface a series of steps, up which we ascended, at an angle deflecting not more than twenty degrees from a vertical line, one hundred and seventy-five feet, to its topmost junction with the rock.

The peril to which this performance exposed us was now fully revealed, and had we seen it at the foot of the ice-sheet, the whole world would not have tempted us to the effort we had made. Why the entire mass of ice, yielding to our exertions, was not detached from its slender fastenings and hurled down the mountain is a mystery. On looking down through the space which separated it from the rock, I could see half a dozen icy tentacles, all of small size, reaching from wall to wall.

Seemingly the weight of a bird would have loosened the entire field. We felt, as we planted our feet on the solid mountain, that we had escaped a great peril—and quenching our thirst from one of the numerous little rivulets which trickled down the rock, set resolutely at work to clamber over the fragments and piles of granite which lay between us and the summit. This was more tedious than difficult, but we were amply rewarded when, at three o'clock P.M., after ten hours of the severest labor of my life, we stepped upon the highest point of the Grand Teton. Man measures his triumphs by the toil and exposure incurred in the attainment of them. We felt that we had achieved a victory, and that it was something for ourselves to know—a solitary satisfaction—that we were the first white men who had ever stood upon the spot we then occupied. Others might come after us, but to be the first where a hundred had failed was no braggart boast.

Central Teton Range through willows.

The several pinnacles of the Grand Teton seen from the valley seem of equal height, but the inequality in this respect was very apparent at the top. The main summit, separated by erosions from the surrounding knobs, embraced an irregular area of thirty by forty feet. Exposure to the winds kept it free from snow and ice, and its bald, denuded head was worn smooth by the elemental warfare waged around it. With the unshorn beams of summer sun shining full upon us, we were obliged to don our overcoats for protection against the cold mountain breeze. Indeed, so light was the atmosphere, that our respiration from its frequency became almost burdensome, and we experienced, in no slight degree, how at such an elevation one could at a single exposure suffer the opposite intensities of heat and cold. Above the ice-belt, over which we had made such a perilous ascent, we saw in the débris the fresh track of that American Ibex, the mountain sheep,—the only animal known to clamber up the sides of our loftiest peaks. Flowers also, of beauteous hue, and delicate fragrance, peeped through the snow, where-ever a rocky jut had penetrated the ice surface.

On the top of an adjacent pinnacle, but little lower than the one we occupied, we found a circular enclosure, six feet in diameter, composed of granite slabs, set up endwise, about five feet in height. It was evidently intended, by whomsoever built, as a protection against the wind, and we were only too glad to avail ourselves of it while we finished our luncheon. On entering it we found ourselves a foot deep in the detritus, which had been worn by the canker of time from the surrounding walls. The great quantity of this substance bore evidence to the antiquity of the structure.

Facing page: Bulk elk under Teton ramparts.

Evidently the work of the Indians, it could not have been constructed less than a century ago, and it is not improbable that its age may reach back for many centuries. A period of time which human experience cannot calculate, was require to produce this wonderful disintegration of solid granite. It was the great wonder of our day's work, and proved that even the Indians, usually so incurious, had some time been influenced by the same spirit which had inspired us....

Far away on the northern horizon, scarcely distinguishable from the clouds with which they are intermingled, we saw the Belt, Madison and Main Rocky ranges, from which long, lateral spurs stretch down on either side, and close up the immense amphitheater by uniting with the Malade Range on the south. Within this vast enclosure, and more immediately beneath us, we overlooked the valley of the Snake, the emerald surface of Pierre's Hole with its mountain surroundings, the dark defile leading into Jackson's Hole, and Jackson and De Lacy lakes, Madison Lake, the source of the Snake River,—Henry's Lake, the source of the North Fork, and afar off, beyond these, the cloud defined peaks of the Wind River mountains, and the peaks surrounding the great lake of Yellowstone. Our elevation was so great that the valley beneath us, filled as it was with knobs and cañons and foot-hills, had the appearance of a vast and level plain, stretching away to, and imperceptibly blending with the distance mountains.

We gazed upon the varied beauties of this wondrous panorama until reminded by the position of the sun that we had scarcely time to effect our descent, and return to

"After ten hours of the severest labor of my life, we stepped upon the highest point of the Grand Teton." PHOTO BY DAN HUHN

COMING DOWN THE MOUNTAIN

camp before dark. Great caution was necessary while passing down the ice belt lest it should become detached, but it was our only passage-way to the bottom, and we were greatly relieved when we reached in safety the cranny occupied by Hamp and Spencer. At this point Captain Stevenson separated from us, and was the first to reach the base of the mountain. We clambered over the rocks and precipices with all possible expedition, and stood in safety upon the saddle, just as the sun was setting.

The interval between sunset and evening in these high latitudes is very brief, and we had yet to descend the ridge. In our haste to accomplish this we selected a pathway between ledges too abrupt to scale, which led directly to a precipice, thirty-five feet in height, at the base of which was a mass of granite fragments and débris from three to four feet deep. We were now in a dilemma. Either we must pass the declivity or re-ascend the steep mountain side, five hundred feet or more, and select another passage. Crawling to the edge, I saw at a distance of twenty feet a jutting point, which would afford standing room for a single person, and about eight feet below it, a small projection, too sharp on the face for a safe foothold. Passing the rope alternately around the bodies of my comrades, I let them down the perpendicular wall to the base, then throwing the middle of the rope over a projecting crag, and seizing the two ends, I lowered myself to the narrow shelf first described, whence a well directed leap enabled me to poise myself on the smaller projection below, and gather for a final jump into the pile of débris, where my comrades stood. Our safe descent being thus accomplished, we had yet the snow-fields, ridges, and gorges

Facing page: Afternoon turbulence.

to traverse, before we arrived in camp. Fatigued with the exercise of ascending and descending the Teton, the passage of these ridges was the most exhaustive effort of our lives. It was after nine o'clock, and very dark, when we first caught sight of our camp fire, afar down the chasm. After a rough walk over prostrate trunks, through deep depressions, amid pine thickets, climbing bowlders, penetrating chapparal, wading streams,—at just thirty minutes past ten, when all our comrades had thought some serious and perhaps fatal accident had befallen us, we entered camp amid cordial greetings and shouts of delight. The joy of a re-union, after even so brief a separation, was as earnest and sincere as if we had been parted a year. ◆

"The interval between sunset and evening in these high latitudes is very brief."

82

Left: Pelican at Colter Bay.

Facing page: Surprise Lake.

Following pages: Daybreak brings new explorations.

Bull elk, Mt. Teewinot.